Original title:

Beneath the Palm Trees

Copyright © 2025 Creative Arts Management OÜ

All rights reserved.

Author: Julian Montgomery

ISBN HARDBACK: 978-1-80581-474-0

ISBN PAPERBACK: 978-1-80581-001-8

ISBN EBOOK: 978-1-80581-474-0

Sun-Kissed Serenity

With shades on and a drink in hand,
I plan my great escape to sand.
The sun is bright, it warms my toes,
While seagulls squawk and steal my pose.

I flip and flop like floppy fish,
While dreaming loudly of my wish.
A nap, a snack, then fun galore,
The beach is calling—who could ask for more!

Lagoon Dreams

Sipping smoothies by the shore,
Where laughter rings and sea waves roar.
I see a crab with dance moves slick,
But trip and fall—oh, what a trick!

With mermaids dancing near the reef,
I join the party, what a relief!
Fish eye me with a curious glance,
As I flail about in my silly dance.

Dancing with the Winds

The breeze is cheeky, it hugs my face,
I chase my hat, it's quite the race.
I tumble over, roll in delight,
The sand gets cozy with my plight.

A pelican joins, with style so grand,
He squawks out jokes; they're simply bland.
But I can't stop, I'm too far gone,
With laughter ringing till the dawn!

Oasis of Tranquility

In a hammock, oh so fine,
I swing and sip my drink divine.
A lizard passes with a wink,
As I ponder life while I sink.

The sun sets low while I eat fries,
With squirrels plotting their surprise.
They scurry up for crumbs galore,
While I just grin and ask for more!

Retreat to the Swaying Heights

In a place where coconuts fall,
I tried to catch one, but missed it all.
The birds above, they laugh and tease,
As I trip on roots and struggle with ease.

The hammock sways, I'm feeling grand,
Until I spill my drink in the sand.
Laughter echoes through the breeze,
As I dance and trip with sheer unease.

The sunset glows, a fiery show,
I set my drink down, oh no, oh no!
A crab appears, with sneaky intent,
And makes off with snacks I never meant.

So here I lounge, with sunburned skin,
Telling tales of my clumsy win.
With laughter echoing through the night,
In this retreat, everything feels right.

Sylvan Secrets of the Sunlit Cove

A squirrel chatted, quite the chap,
As I napped beneath my sunburnt cap.
It begged my sandwich, saying, "Please!"
I wish I'd packed some extra cheese!

The waves roll in with a cheeky splash,
My towel takes off, oh what a dash!
I run after it, like a clumsy fool,
While onlookers chuckle, I play the fool.

Sunshine tickles, the ice cream melts,
My hands, anew, with sticky svelte.
A seagull swoops, my cone's no more,
Guess he's the boss, I just adore!

So here we float, in this silly dance,
With salty chips and a sun-kissed chance.
Laughter rings in the vibrant air,
In this cove of fun, with joy to spare!

Festivities of the Green Canopy

In a leafy spot, we dance and sway,
Laughter echoes, come what may.
Monkeys join, they steal the show,
With their antics, we laugh and glow.

Cocktails served in coconut cups,
While the breeze playfully interrupts.
Swaying fronds toss confetti high,
As sunny rays tickle the sky.

A Tapestry in Turquoise Hues

Waves crash softly upon bright sands,
With sandy toes and water in hands.
Seagulls gossip, sharing the news,
While we sip our fuchsia fruit brews.

In the shade, wild tales unfold,
Of sunburnt noses and drinks too bold.
A crab in a hat struts with pride,
As we take bets on his wild ride.

Canvas of the Coastal Dawn

Morning breaks with laughter alive,
As sleepy heads start to thrive.
A parrot squawks, 'Rise and shine!'
While we brew the coffee divine.

With breakfast spread on banana leaves,
We toast to friends and ocean eaves.
As waves giggle at our chatter,
And fish below are in on the matter.

Rejuvenation in a Tropical Oasis

In this oasis, time stands still,
With breezy laughs and a sun-kissed thrill.
We play games that make no sense,
While sipping drinks, a sweet recompense.

Swaying hammocks catch our dreams,
As we plot out the next wild schemes.
A turtle's race with a slow-motion twist,
And we cheer it on, none can resist!

Rituals of the Sea Breeze

The seagulls squawk in silly glee,
As beach bums roll from sea to spree.
In sandcastles high, a brave knight's plea,
While flip-flops dance with such esprit.

A crab in shades struts with panache,
Holding a drink, oh what a splash!
He's got moves, that little rascal,
Challenging waves to a wacky clash.

Nightfall in the Palm Grove

The lanterns flicker, fireflies beguile,
While islanders sway in a dreamy style.
With coconut shells, we laugh and smile,
As the moon grins wide with a cheeky dial.

A parrot cracks jokes in squawky tones,
We dance like dervishes, forgetting our phones.
With laughter echoing, the night alone,
Our spirits soar, like windblown stones.

Island Whispers

In tides of laughter, secrets float,
A turtle winks in a funny coat.
He tells tall tales of a royal boat,
While starfish giggle, striking a pose.

A llama in shades sips salty tea,
Saying, "Life's too short, choose sandy glee!"
With wind in my hair, I shout with glee,
As the beach bum brigade joins the spree.

The Heart of the Bahamas

With conch shells trumpeting our cheer,
We dance to rhythms, loud and clear.
A fish in a tuxedo swims near,
Threatening to steal our lunch, oh dear!

A hammock sways with a squeaky song,
While we invite laughter all night long.
In the heart of fun where we belong,
Each wave reminds us we can do no wrong.

Twilight Under the Tropics

In the dimming light, a lizard strays,
Chasing after shadows, in comical ways.
The crickets tune up, they sing in delight,
While I'm just a mess, caught in the night.

A coconut drops, thumping my head,
I laugh at the palm trees, pretending they said,
"Just hang out with us, we're really quite fun!"
As I chuckle and roll, under the sun.

A Haven of Hush

In the quiet cocoon where the sun softly beams,
Squirrels make mischief, fulfilling their dreams.
A hammock sways gently, a little too low,
I tumble right out, what a glorious show!

The ocean whispers secrets, waves slapping the shore,
I try to keep quiet, but my giggles roar.
A sand crab considers a race with my toe,
I bid it good luck, but it's too slow!

The Caress of Coastal Breezes

As breezes swoosh past, they pull at my hat,
A seagull swoops down, and I think, "What's that?"
It circles and caws, claiming my snack,
Oh, it won't get away, I dare it to come back!

With each gust of wind, I do a little dance,
My flip-flops fly off, now isn't that a chance?
But laughter erupts, a sun-kissed parade,
Chasing my sandals—a playful charade!

Sunlit Silhouettes

In sunlit silhouettes, the world seems just right,
A trio of tourists, caught in mid-flight.
They tumble and spill, like spilled lemonade,
While I sip my drink, absolutely amazed.

A parrot squawks loud, thinks it's quite a star,
I'm watching these antics, not sure where they are.
With awkward ballet near a beach ball's embrace,
It's the silliest show on this sandy place!

Palm Frond Fantasies

In a shady nook, I saw a cat,
Practicing yoga, all curled like that.
The fronds above, they waved and swayed,
Jealous of the poses my kitty made.

Giggling toucans, ready to tease,
Did a pirouette, with remarkable ease.
I clapped my hands, they squawked with glee,
Sipping on jokes like cool, sweet tea.

Bouncing squirrels in a playful race,
Chased after shadows, oh what a pace!
They thought they won, but oh, surprise,
I had the perfect snack for their eyes.

Laughter echoes through the humid air,
As the sun sets softly, without a care.
Under the fronds, we dance and play,
In the quirky rhythm of the tropical day.

Under the Canopy of Time

A sloth on a branch, taking a snooze,
Woke up to find he'd missed the news.
He stretched his limbs, then looked around,
And wondered why it was so quiet and sound.

A parrot squawked, "It's time for brunch!"
But the sloth just yawned and took a hunch.
"Brunch can wait, I'm having a dream,
Of flying high, or so it would seem."

The monkeys swung by in a jittery spree,
Avoiding the sloth like he carried a flea.
"Hey buddy, don't you want to join?"
But he just grinned and continued his coin.

As time tick-tocked, under leafy screens,
Silliness blossomed in various scenes.
Each laugh a ripple in the humid air,
Where time slowed down, without a care.

Gentle Whispers of the Tropics

A breeze tickles leaves, whispers in jest,
While crabs on the sand put their skills to the test.
One claimed it could run faster than a hare,
But tripped on its claw, causing quite a scare.

Coconuts fell like ungrateful bombs,
Rolling down hills, creating sweet qualms.
An octopus chuckled from the nearby tide,
"Don't worry, little crab, it was quite a ride!"

Lizards in shades, lounging with flair,
Sporting tiny hats, the latest in wear.
They sipped on fresh juice, oh what a show,
Savoring gossip as the breezes blow.

A gecko danced on a branch overhead,
Trying to impress a pigeon instead.
In the tropical haze, we all find our flow,
With laughter and mischief, beneath the grow.

Moonlight's Caress on Silken Sands

At nightfall, crabs waltzed on the beach,
Practicing moves that were out of their reach.
The moonlight chuckled, casting a glow,
On a dance-off that stole quite the show.

A starfish chimed in, with a feisty jig,
Swaying its arms like it was wearing a wig.
"Look at me shine!" it proudly proclaimed,
While the waves giggled softly, playing the game.

Nearby, a clam joined the frolicking spree,
Clapping its shells, trying to be free.
The rhythm wove magic under the sky,
While seagulls circled, singing a lullaby.

As fun filled the air, the tide gently kissed,
Each cheeky shellfish caught in the mist.
In the calm of the night, under starlit bands,
We laughed and we danced, leaving colorful strands.

Coconuts and Summer Solstice

Sipping on a drink that's bright,
Coconuts roll, what a sight!
Birds above begin to squawk,
As we try to take a walk.

Sandy toes and sunburned nose,
Trying hard to dodge the hose.
Friends are laughing, sun is hot,
Oh, did I just lose my spot?

Seems a crab has claimed my chair,
Waving claws, without a care.
We'll just have to switch and swap,
As we enjoy the beach-side hop.

Ice cream cones are melting fast,
Taste of summer, what a blast!
Life is better by the tide,
Laughter's truly amplified.

A Canopy of Calm

Underneath a leafy shade,
We play cards and sip lemonade.
A squirrel steals my sandwich quick,
Maybe he's the ultimate trick?

Laughter echoes through the leaves,
While a passing breeze deceives.
Is it me or did that gust
Just send that lady's hat to dust?

Chasing down the runaway fries,
Flying high like birdy skies.
Each time I bend down to look,
I swear I might just lose my book!

Sunset glows, we wrap it up,
Squirrels dance, no need to fuss.
Filled with joy, we slowly roam,
Where giggles find a place called home.

The Rhythm of Gentle Breezes

Dancing grass, the breeze is light,
Whispers tell of springtime's flight.
Seagulls squawk, they steal the show,
On the sand, we casually tow.

Tiptoe past the crabby clan,
Waving as they make their plan.
Shells and rocks are treasures found,
As we spin in laughter's round.

Tropical tunes and laughter loud,
Join us under nature's crowd.
Sun sets low, the sky's a feast,
So of course, we play at least!

Breeze is teasing with a laugh,
As we all take a little nap.
Ah, what joy this day brings forth,
Laughter echoes, a true mirth's worth!

Haven of Harmony

Under shades of bright green leaves,
Life's simpler, away from thieves.
Dance with shadows, twirl and glide,
Nothing but joy, we refuse to hide.

Laying back with tunes so sweet,
A picnic sprawled, oh what a treat!
Mischief lurks in my friend's eye,
Toward the snacks, they stealthily pry.

Giggles chase the clouds above,
Every moment, filled with love.
Barbeques and jokes in flight,
As day fades into starry night.

Let's toast to life, both bold and bright,
Silly stories, pure delight.
When we gather, peace takes stake,
Hearts in sync, oh the joy we make!

Tranquil Tides and Timeless Vistas

Waves giggle as they crash and play,
Seagulls snicker, swooping away.
Sandy toes and sunburned noses,
Wish we'd brought more chocolate roses.

Fishes tease with a slippery dance,
While crabs plot their next big chance.
We laugh at the sun's silly grin,
Dancing shadows, let the fun begin!

Cradled by Nature's Symphony

Bees buzzing like they're telling jokes,
Even flowers share some pokes.
Butterflies flutter, what a sight,
Winking at us, taking flight.

Trees whisper secrets, oh so sly,
As squirrels giggle, passing by.
Nature's playlist, all tunes divine,
Who's that barking? It's just a pine!

A Blissful Reverie of Greenery

Mossy cushions beneath our feet,
Laughter mingles with nature's beat.
A lizard strikes a modeling pose,
While a snail says, 'Wait till I doze!'

Grass stains on our shirts, oh dear,
But who cares? We're full of cheer!
Nature's playground, we hold the key,
And we're planning a parade, just us three!

Fragrance of Forgotten Flora

Scented petals in a playful twist,
Even the weeds just can't resist.
Dandelions wish to be a star,
While the roses roll their eyes from afar.

The breeze holds laughter, sweet and light,
Bouncing daisies, oh what a sight!
We chase the shadows, giggling loud,
Nature's our stage, and we're so proud!

Poetic Shadows of an Island Breeze

In a hammock swinging low,
I dreamed of fish that wear a bow.
Coconut crabs play chess at dawn,
While parrots sing a silly song.

A sandcastle with a moaty car,
Crab racetrack just a few feet far.
Turtles sneak a cookie break,
As waves giggle and splashes make.

Lizards dance on sun-kissed sand,
Chasing shadows, very grand.
Mermaids whisper, "let's eat pie,"
A seagull swoops and steals my fry!

With a flip-flop full of sand,
I try to walk, it's so unplanned.
Laughing waves, they tease and mock,
As I trip and tumbleock.

Starlit Nights and Gentle Mornings

The moon's a disco ball tonight,
With crickets joining in delight.
The coconuts, they dance around,
As I laugh at my own sound.

Sipping rum from seashells wide,
While starfish stare with dotty pride.
A wiggly worm winks at me,
Says, "Aloha! Care for tea?"

The morning sun's a lazy guy,
With sleepy clouds that float on by.
A parrot lost a mean old joke,
And all the dolphins laughed and poked.

Tanned tourists strut, looking sharp,
While I'm stuck in a coconut harp.
With a splash and a squeal of glee,
I'm just a nut, that's plain to see!

Secrets in the Tropical Night

At twilight, secrets rise and flow,
Like dancing salsa, don't you know?
The shadows tell of coconuts' schemes,
While iguanas plot their evening dreams.

A crab in shades, so stylishly neat,
Challenges me to a conch shell feat.
The bonfire crackles, laughter swells,
As fish tell tales of ancient spells.

Under the stars, with piña coladas,
We ponder life and silly banters.
A palm leaf swoops to steal my hat,
And now I've lost my witty spat.

With every wave that tickles my toes,
The rhythm of night in chuckles grows.
As sleep creeps in, with laughter tight,
I dream of crabs, and what's secret tonight.

Rhapsody of Rustling Leaves

Leaves are clapping, what a show!
Cheeky monkeys jump to and fro.
A toucan's hat, quite out of line,
Sips juice from an oversized lime.

The coconut's running, it's got some sass,
Tumbling down the hill, oh what a class!
Fishy friends are doing a jig,
While I just try to dance, oh dig!

As the sunlight bows, day's almost done,
Squirrels sing songs of their own fun.
The rustling whispers giggle and tease,
A light-footed breeze brings out the knees.

So here's to laughter, and some good cheer,
With grinning friends, we hold them dear.
In this island beat, we find our way,
With rustling leaves, we dance and play.

Odyssey of Ocean and Earth

Sandcastles rise, a wobbly feat,
Jellyfish dance, they wiggle and greet.
A crab in a tux, with a pinch of a snare,
Whispers of secrets, caught in the air.

A seagull's laugh, it's a cheeky song,
Waves crash and tumble, where do they belong?
Surfboards wobble, like socks on a line,
In this sandy saga, we're building our shrine.

Seeking Shelter from the World

A hammock sways, it's calling my name,
Zebras in flip-flops, oh what a game!
Sunburned dolphins with shades on their nose,
Ask if I'd trade for a life made of prose.

Old coconut heads, they gossip for fun,
Plotting the next prank under the sun.
Palm fronds chuckle, with secrets to tell,
While I sip coconut milk, oh do it so well!

Laughter and Light in Isles of Gold

A treasure map scribbled on the back of a shoe,
Baboons in bandanas, what mischief they brew.
Sandy toes shuffling, a mermaid's ballet,
Fish flashing smiles, they join in the play.

Upside-down pineapples, hats for the sun,
Dance like nobody; oh, what fun!
With ticklish seashells underfoot,
In this island kingdom, all worries are mute.

Nature's Embrace of Bright Horizons

A parrot in spectacles reads news of the bay,
While turtles discuss how to frolic all day.
Winds that are giggling, they tussle my hair,
Sunset spaghetti, with time to spare.

Fields of daffodils, all dressed in their best,
Invite me for tea, it's a whimsical quest.
Balloons made of clouds float over the coast,
In this wild laughter, I cherish the most.

The Lullaby of Fragrant Breezes

In the shade where no one cares,
A monkey steals my fruity pears.
The breeze brings laughter, sweet and light,
As we nap through day and party at night.

The tickle of sand on my toes,
Crab runs by with his funny poses.
Seagulls squawk, they want my fries,
While I dream of coconut pies.

A parrot yells the latest news,
'It's snack time folks!' Oh, what a muse!
The hammock swings, I feel so fine,
With breezy whispers and sweet sunshine.

As the stars start winking high,
A turtle waves as he crawls by.
In this tropical hideaway bliss,
Every little moment, I surely won't miss.

Nestled in Nature's Embrace

Coconuts fall with a thud and clap,
While tourists here set up their nap.
Laughter echoes near the shore,
As gulls steal snacks — we shout for more!

Banana peels become a slide,
The kids all giggle, full of pride.
A race to see who can run fast,
But slip and slide — oh what a blast!

The palm leaves sway in a silly dance,
We mingle, laugh, hide, and prance.
The gift shop sells outrageous hats,
And I pretend I'm a giant cat!

At sunset, drinks with little umbrellas,
We toast to life, to silly fella.
In this cozy, nature's embrace,
Every laugh is a warm embrace.

Stories Spoken by the Sea

Waves tell tales with a foamy grin,
Of a fish that dreamed of being a king.
The crabs do the cha-cha in the sand,
While the shells chuckle, hot off land.

Octopus with ink so bright,
Paints the ocean, a dazzling sight.
He writes love notes in deep blue,
That only mermaids can pursue.

Seashells gossip, oh what a scene,
Of a dolphin's dance, so sleek and keen.
With laughter as the ocean's tune,
They twirl and frolic beneath the moon.

A turtle tells the slowest jokes,
While the fishy crew just croaks and pokes.
In this splashy, watery spree,
The sea brings smiles, wild and free.

Twilight Tales of Tropical Comfort

Once the sun dips low and shy,
The fireflies dance, oh my, oh my!
Roasting marshmallows, sweet delight,
As friends craft stories given flight.

The ukulele strums a merry tune,
While crickets join, a charming croon.
Flashlights flicker, shadows play,
As we share secrets of the day.

A lizard in a bowtie struts,
He steals the spotlight, what a nut!
With jokes about his fancy flair,
He leaves us laughing without a care.

As the stars spill stories so grand,
We cozy up, hand in hand.
In twilight's glow, we find our bliss,
Each silly tale, a gentle kiss.

Flickers of Joy Amidst the Greens

In the shade where shadows play,
A monkey swipes my snack away.
Laughter bubbles, bright as sun,
   Guess I'm not the only one!

Swinging limbs, quite the show,
A lizard darts, oh, where'd he go?
   With sporadic steps I dance,
   But trip over my own pants!

Sipping drinks with little umbrellas,
   Finding shells to tell the fellas.
Crab races on the sandy ground,
   Epic battles yet to be found!

Jokes exchanged 'neath leafy crowd,
While gardeners sing a lullaby loud.
Here, mirth blooms in wild array,
   Brightening up our sunny day!

Where the Sand Meets the Sea

Waves do the cha-cha on the shore,
Seagulls cackling, wanting more.
I noted down my grand beach plan,
But now I'm stuck, half-buried man!

Sandcastles rise, a grand mistake,
Flimsy towers begin to shake.
Buckets spill and laughter reigns,
I lose my hat to salty gains!

Tanning lotion, missed my back,
Now I look like a lobster, lack!
With squawks and giggles all around,
We're the silliest folks in town!

Frisbees fly, and umbrellas bend,
Days like these, they never end.
Chasing sunsets, grains of gold,
Making memories, truth be told!

Lost in Sunlit Serenity

Chasing shadows, sun is bright,
Stumbling over flip-flop flight.
Coconuts crack, laughter spills,
Life is full of funny thrills!

A hammock sways with graceful ease,
Catching naps when I feel the breeze.
But then I wake, and oh, what fun!
Turns out, I napped beneath the sun!

Colorful drinks with straws so long,
Sip too fast, and it feels wrong.
Tropical fruits, a feast divine,
Mango madness; it's all mine!

Under the sun, we joke and tease,
Falling over with such great ease.
Here among each giggling friend,
These bright days, we'll never end!

Conversations Under the Tropical Sky

Beneath the waves, tales untold,
With crabs that boast, so bold, so bold.
Chatting with parrots, what a scene,
They squawk back, nearly obscene!

Umbrellas tilt, drinks overflow,
Discussing fashion with a toadstool crow.
"Is this shirt too bright?" I ask with flair,
He caws back, "Wear with care!"

Under the sun, secrets shared,
With dancing palms, we're unprepared.
Giggling fits at every glance,
Life becomes a silly dance.

As the sun dips low and wide,
We toast to fun, with smiles of pride.
Here we'll linger, laughter high,
In our joyful, tropical sky!

Echoes of the Endless Sky

In a land where coconuts drop,
Sandy burials, right at the top.
Seagulls cackle, they steal my chips,
My old sun hat, it flips and flips.

With sunburn stripes quite like a zebra,
I sip my drink and strut like a diva.
A crab scuttles past, a crafty thief,
While I'm left with salty relief.

The ocean giggles, it's a funny scene,
As waves crash down with a frothy sheen.
My flip-flops fly in a silly dance,
What's life without a little chance?

The sunset paints the sky so wide,
Time to collect my lunchbox tide.
Tomorrow, I swear, I'll pack it tight,
But who could resist this beachy flight?

Harmonies of the Ocean's Edge

The waves come in with a playful cheer,
While seashells whisper, 'Come grab a beer!'
My towel's a stage for a crab ballet,
As seagulls jest in their funny ballet.

A dolphin winks at my goofy hat,
While I'm busy fighting a rogue beach rat.
The breeze hums along to a comic tune,
As sand sticks to me like a clingy raccoon.

A kid nearby launches a mean ice cream,
It lands on my friend—oh, what a dream!
We laugh till we cry in this sun-drenched land,
With sticky fingers and a melted hand.

The horizon glows in peachy delight,
Under stars that blink, oh what a night!
With friends like these, how can it be grim?
Life's a joke, and the punchline's a whim!

Evoking Essence in the Hum of Nature

Buzzing insects join in the fun,
While I swat and laugh, oh what a run!
A lizard sunbathes on a nearby stone,
While I tumble over, claiming my throne.

The palm fronds whisper secrets and lies,
As the sun sets low in the painted skies.
I trip on a root, now that's just fine,
Nature laughs with me in a comedy line.

The breeze carries smells of sweet coconut,
But the only thing here is my big old rut.
I thought I'd impress with a fancy move,
Instead, I'm imitating a sloth groove.

So here's to the moments, both silly and bright,
With each goofy laugh and each playful fright.
I'll dance with the shadows and frolic with glee,
In the laughter of nature, I truly feel free!

Dance of the Tropical Twilight

As night descends like a soft old quilt,
I kick off my shoes, for fun's been built.
With fireflies twinkling like cosmic jesters,
I join the dance, no time for testers.

A coconut drinks from my bloated cup,
While a tropical breeze gives me a sup.
The stars above roll their eyes and shine,
Watching us dance like we're sipping on wine.

The roaches chime in with their tiny tap,
While I lose my balance and plop on a lap.
A parrot squawks out, 'Now that's a sight!'
We've turned a kitchen into delightful night.

A conga line weaves through the sand and grass,
With laughter echoing in a merry mass.
As twilight wraps up the last of the fun,
I think we've finally fried in the sun!

Whispers of the Fronds

In the shade of a leafy crown,
Lizards dance, not a care, not a frown.
Coconuts drop with a thud so loud,
While crabs strut around, feeling proud.

A toucan laughs from high up above,
Chasing squirrels, they swoop with a shove.
With a wink of a leaf, the wind plays tricks,
As sunburned tourists do their best flips.

Bananas giggle as monkeys swing,
Spreading cheer like it's a big fling.
Oh, how the palms sway with tease and grace,
A comedy show, nature's funny place.

And when night falls, under glittering stars,
The fireflies flash like tiny guitars.
The crickets sing a tune of delight,
While we sip a drink, giggling all night.

Shadows on the Sand

Footprints dance on the golden shore,
A seagull swoops like an aerial chore.
Kids run wild, splashing around,
While mom drops her hat—what a comical sound!

A crab with swagger, moving with flair,
Snatches a snack without a care.
As waves laugh along, tickling toes,
The sun overheats, but nobody knows.

With sandcastles built to scrappy perfection,
A brave dog arrives, all paws and direction.
He knocks them down, what a sight to see!
A royal disaster, oh, such glee!

And finally, as the sun dips low,
We question the shell that should definitely glow.
The laughter subsides, as we wave goodbye,
To shadows that stretch 'neath a brightening sky.

Swaying in the Breeze

Whiskers twitch as the breeze blows sweet,
A gecko clings with nimble little feet.
Wobbly tables on picnic days,
As sandwiches dance in the light of rays.

The juice dribbles down a chin so bright,
While laughter erupts at the first big bite.
The wind carries hiccups into the air,
While ants make plans — they're quite the pair!

With laughter shared over board games played,
Water fights break out, none are dismayed.
Sunburns develop in odd, funny shapes,
As we roll on the ground, just a bunch of apes!

As dusk wraps us in a blanket of pink,
The kids start to plot, and we barely blink.
To catch fireflies is the goal so bold,
But all we catch are giggles, oh, so gold!

A Tapestry of Green

In a jungle gym of twisting vines,
Chameleons wave like they're in the lines.
A sloth takes a nap, snoring so loud,
While monkeys fancy themselves quite proud.

The toucan's beak curves like a bright rainbow,
As he tells all the gossip, oh, don't you know?
Squirrels throw acorns in the wildest games,
Their laughter echoes, so wild it tames.

Frogs leap high, making splashes so cute,
While hummingbirds zoom past in pursuit.
What a circus, oh, what a spree,
In the fabric of life, so vibrant and free!

As the sun dips slowly, painting the sky,
The ululation of crickets pulls a sigh.
In this tapestry, laughter entwines,
With each little creature, joy always shines.

Coastal Castles Made of Dreams

In the sand, we built a throne,
With seashells and stones, we made it known.
A seagull squawked, claimed our crown,
Now we're just royalty wearing a frown.

Our moat is just a splash so near,
As crabs parade, they bring us cheer.
The tide came in, took our flags,
Our castle shrunk, oh the funny gags!

We fought with waves, they laughed back hard,
Paddling out while wearing our bard.
Each mighty wave, we tried to conquer,
Ended up drenched, oh, what a bonker!

We'll build again, our dreams in sight,
With a bucket and spade, we'll take flight.
But first, let's snack on chips with glee,
Building castles, just you and me!

Treasures of a Tropical Realm

A treasure map drawn in melted ice,
Glimmers of gold, we roll the dice.
At the X, a beach ball we found,
Our pirate dreams, forever bound.

The coconut drinks, they overflow,
Drunk on juice, we dance in a row.
The crabby crew starts a conga line,
With shells for hats, all feeling fine.

A parrot on our shoulder, squawking loud,
Says, 'Join the fun!'—and we feel proud.
Dancing like no one's around,
Finding treasures in laughter, profound.

Though the loot was only some old flip-flops,
We shared a joke, and the fun never stops.
In the realm of sun, we savor delight,
With treasures of joy, we take flight!

Nature's Repose in Tropical Hues

The sun shakes hands with ocean's tide,
While squirrels in shades put on a ride.
Hammocks sway, with laughter and snores,
Nature's nap, who could ask for more?

In vivid greens, the iguanas play,
Trying to blend in, but we see them sway.
We giggle at their sunbathing style,
With goofy poses that make us smile.

The palm fronds whisper tales of fun,
In a language that tells of a little run.
Banana peels become a playful slide,
Nature's waterpark, come take a ride!

So we rejoice in this cozy nook,
With squirrels and shadows, let's write a book.
Each chuckle shared beneath the shade,
In hues of joy, our worries fade!

Embracing the Ocean's Serenade

The waves hum tunes, like rock bands play,
While beach balls bounce and dogs find sway.
Seagulls try to join in the jam,
But they're tone-deaf—oh, what a sham!

The beach is our stage, we dance like stars,
In flip-flops that squeak, we're who we are.
With every wave crashing down like a beat,
We tumble and laugh, landing on our feet.

In sun hats and shades, we're fashionably late,
Strutting our stuff, we just can't wait.
A sandcastle fit for a king or queen,
Rising up high, oh, what a scene!

So here's to the joy in every splash,
To the silly moments, we just won't stash.
Embracing the rhythm of days so fine,
Where laughter and waves perfectly align!

The Allure of Whispering Winds

The wind tickles my nose,
As I chase a lizard's toes.
It darts here and there,
While I run with flair.

A coconut falls with a thud,
I slip on mud and land with a stud.
A parrot squawks, "Are you okay?"
I reply, "Best tumble of the day!"

The breeze carries giggles near,
Those monkeys have too much cheer.
Swinging around like they're on a spree,
I wonder if they'll invite me for tea!

A hammock calls with a gentle sway,
I bounce and roll, oh what a play!
The sun waves down with a wink,
Even palm fronds seem to think!

Journeying Through Sunlit Shades

Walking in light, with snacks galore,
I spot a crab along the shore.
It dances sideways, quite a sight,
I laugh and say, "You're a delight!"

A beach ball flies past my head,
And lands on a sunbathing bed.
An old man snorts, says, "Well, that's new!"
I grin, it's aiming right for you!

In the shade, a game of cards,
With colorful drinks and funny guards.
I lose my shirt to a rummy bet,
At least it's sunny, not a threat!

As the sun sinks low in the sky,
I spot a seal with a pastry pie.
It winks at me, quite the tease,
And I can't help but laugh with ease!

Beneath a Canopy of Dreams

In a hammock, I do sway,
Dreaming of snacks, oh what a day!
With a cool breeze in my hair,
I feel like I haven't a care.

A bird flew by with a funny hat,
I wondered, "What's up with that?"
It strutted like the star of the show,
And I chuckled as it stole the glow.

I tried meditating, found my zen,
But a goat showed up with my pen.
It chewed it slowly, looked so sly,
This little guy is my new ally!

Soon the stars twinkle above,
I giggle as they whisper of love.
For every laugh and every cheer,
This paradise holds magic, it's clear.

Flourishing in the Tropics

In gardens lush, where sweet scents play,
I trip on a vine while on my way.
Flowers shout, "Watch your step!"
I laugh and say, "Don't be inept!"

A turtle joins my dance routine,
With moves so slow, it's a quirky scene.
We laugh and groove on the warm ground,
Making up moves that are quite profound!

A fruit bat swoops down with flair,
Wearing shades, no signs of care.
I shout, "Hey buddy, where's your style?"
It grins and tails my goofy smile!

Even the sand seems to grin,
As I tumble in with a big spin.
In this world, each moment gleams,
Full of laughter, bursting dreams!

Island Dreams and Sunlit Skies

The piña colada spills on my toes,
Seagulls laugh as the beach ball goes.
Waves tickle my feet, oh what a treat,
Sandy snacks make for a fun little feast.

Bright flip-flops fly through the air,
Sunburned noses and salty hair.
Tanning naps turn into wild dreams,
Where nothing's as silly as it seems.

Finding a crab out for a stroll,
He glances my way, what's his goal?
With a wink and a claw, off he scuttles,
While I giggle at my own silly struggles.

Ice cream cones melt down my hand,
I chase the drips like a little child planned.
Oh, island life, so carefree and bright,
Where laughter echoes under the sunlight!

The Dance of Dappled Light

Under the leaves, shadows play tricks,
Lizards dance with their quick little kicks.
Sunbeams smile, bright and gold,
While laughter's stories are happily told.

A tropical breeze gives my hair a whirl,
And my drink's a new dance, a silly swirl.
Flip-flops clap as I bust a groove,
Who said being grown-up means I can't move?

Even the palm fronds sway in the fun,
Gossiping softly, 'Oh look, here she comes!'
Nature's own rhythm, the fun never ceases,
In this green kingdom, joy never decreases.

As the sun sets, colors start to blend,
Dancing on waves as if they could bend.
Wrap me in laughter, sun-soaked delight,
For tomorrow's antics are just out of sight!

Coconut Conversations

Two coconuts perched on a sunny ledge,
Discussing life over a fruity pledge.
One cracks jokes while the other rolls eyes,
'You'd think we'd tire, but this is our prize!'

'Hey mate, fancy a trip to the bar?'
'Only if they serve fruit with a jar!'
Monty, the mocktail, winks with delight,
While beach umbrellas sway left and right.

A breeze comes by that shakes up the chat,
'Is it me, or did that seagull just spat?'
Green husks giggle, they can't help but tease,
Sharing tales of the waves and the cheese.

As day drifts slowly into the night,
Coconut friends are a marvelous sight.
For every sip tells a tale oh so grand,
In our little paradise, hand in hand.

Swaying Sentinels

Tall green giants so proud and tall,
Watching over beachgoers, one and all.
They gossip the stories of all who roam,
And shade us sweetly, calling us home.

Twisting the breeze with their leafy dance,
'Hey look, that kid is in a wild prance!'
Kites and kooks whirl beneath their gaze,
While all around, sunlight plays in a haze.

Whispers float through the rustling leaves,
'Did you see that splash? Oh, what a tease!'
They chuckle softly, their laughter grows,
As the sun dips down, a burnished glow shows.

Guardians of giggles and secrets untold,
They tickle our thoughts, and never grow old.
In this colorful world where we play and sway,
Life is a carnival, oh, what a day!

Serenity in the Shadows

In a patch of shade we sneak,
Sipping drinks, feeling unique.
The sun blares down, we squint and grumble,
While all around, the seagulls tumble.

Cool breezes tease the sweaty brow,
We laugh and joke, no need to bow.
A coconut falls, it makes a bang,
We jump and squeal, then hear a clang.

Friends in laughter, life's a breeze,
In this quirky spot, we do what we please.
The fruit flies dance, the ants parade,
Yet in this chaos, joy won't fade.

With every sip we share a tale,
Of sunburns bright and limbs that flail.
So let the jokes roll, as waves lap the sand,
In shadows of joy, we'll ever stand.

Memories Wrapped in Greenery

Wrapped in leaves, we made a den,
Crafted dreams with our own pen.
Under vines, we laughed and played,
While the world outside slowly frayed.

Fruits of laughter, juicy and bright,
We shared our secrets, pure delight.
Mangoes dripping, sticky hands,
This is the fun that understands.

The lizards dash, the crickets sing,
To nature's rhythm, we're the kings.
In every corner, laughter twirls,
As we enjoy this dance of swirls.

With sun-kissed moments, we won't forget,
Each silly story, a perfect set.
So let's rejoice in the shade and cheer,
For every memory, we hold dear!

Shadows on the Shore

Footprints left in golden sand,
With giggles bright, it's unplanned.
A splash of waves, we leap and shout,
As high tide offers a playful bout.

Driftwood games and silly poses,
Sandcastles grow, and sometimes dozes.
But watch your step, a wave's a creep,
We yell and laugh; they cut so deep!

Seagulls squawk, our snacks are thieved,
By crafty beaks, we can't believe.
Yet laughter drowns the salty tears,
In shores, we battle our silly fears.

With every wave, a new delight,
Our sandy suits a comical sight.
The shadows stretch, the sun dips low,
As friends roll in laughter's echo.

Whispered Secrets in the Breeze

In the air, our giggles fly,
As whispers dance and dreams go by.
The breeze carries tales from old,
Of sunburns and adventures bold.

Beneath a tree, we share our dreams,
Cracking jokes, bursting at the seams.
The shadows play their sneaky game,
While wind chimes chime our secret name.

Lost in thoughts of silly things,
Like awkward crushes and rubber rings.
As nature laughs right back at us,
We find ourselves— it's a must!

With every cackle, the sun bows low,
In whispered rumbles, our faces glow.
For in this breeze, we are truly free,
Our secrets held in nature's glee.

The Language of Palm Fronds

Fronds whisper secrets in the breeze,
Telling tales of coconut thieves.
Swaying softly, a leafy dance,
They gossip about the local romance.

With every rustle, a chuckle grows,
As crabs march by in their clumsy shows.
They plot and plan beneath the shade,
While sunburned tourists serenade.

Laughter rings from the ocean's foam,
Even the seashells feel like home.
In every shadow, a joke to share,
Life at play without a care.

The breeze is light, the laughter loud,
As fronds sway in a goofy crowd.
Nature's humor in palm-leafed attire,
Telling jokes that never tire.

Secrets in the Sunlight

Sunlight sparkles on the ocean's face,
While seagulls compete in a race.
Flip-flops fly with a careless grace,
As beach balls bounce in a warm embrace.

Crab races and shouts, oh what a sight!
Even the sand thinks it's day and night.
Bikini tops lost in the fray,
A laugh erupts, come what may.

Jellyfish jelly in a quirky prank,
A surfboard tumbles, the water's rank.
Laughter and splashes, the day is bright,
As friends get tangled in pure delight.

Underneath the blissful sun,
The quirks of summer have just begun.
Each ray a joke, each wave a cheer,
We smile and giggle, year after year.

Drifting Through Green Dreams

In a hammock swaying like a lazy bee,
I dream of snacks and a cool iced tea.
A lizard struts just like a king,
Dressed in green and ready to sing.

The gusts of wind toss my hat away,
As I chuckle at nature's silly play.
A parrot squawks, "You call that a song?"
While laughter echoes all day long.

Tropical vibes and sunscreen fights,
Making shapes with kites and kites.
Lost flip-flops tell quite the tale,
As I trip and tumble, oh, what a fail!

With ridiculous poses, I try to pose,
While a crab scuttles and follows my toes.
Joy drifts in dreamlike apocalypse,
Just laughing at life's funny slips.

Melodies of the Island

Ukuleles strum under the bright sun,
As friends gather, and we all have fun.
Tropical birds join in the beat,
Tipping their hats, oh, what a treat!

Dancing shadows across the sand,
With oddball moves perfectly planned.
Even the coconuts start to sway,
Quite the party, hip-hip hooray!

A joke flies by, like an errant kite,
As we cheer for surfboards in mid-flight.
Each splash a laugh, each grin a song,
In the rhythm of life, we all belong.

So let's toast to beautiful mischief,
With laughter sweeter than any gift.
In every note, every twist of fate,
Melodies sweet, oh, it's never too late!

Secrets of the Tropics

In the shade where coconuts sway,
Monkeys plot their fun and play.
They steal my hat, they steal my drink,
I laugh so hard, I cannot think.

Limes roll free, the drinks get mixed,
A parrot squawks, has me perplexed.
He joins the party, steals the show,
With dance moves that are quite the glow.

Sunshine's bright, yet I must say,
The sunscreen's thick, it's here to stay.
I slip and slide, oh what a sight,
Like fish out of water, in broad daylight.

Secrets whispered, a breeze so sly,
Laughter echoes, a cheerful cry.
In this paradise, craziness flows,
With every step, more giggles grow.

Echoes of the Shoreline

Waves keep crashing, a funny dance,
A crab scuttles, no second chance.
It pinches my toe, oh what a thrill,
I hop and scream, then roll down the hill.

Seagulls dive for snacks on a whim,
While I juggle snacks, my balance is slim.
A sandwich flies, the gulls declare,
As I sit laughing, without a care.

Tin cans and laughter fill the air,
Beach balls soaring, without a care.
We chase our dreams, as tides come and go,
All while planning our next funny show.

Echoes of the shoreline call us near,
In giggles and grins, we find our cheer.
With every wave, a memory grows,
In this sandy world, hilarity flows.

Rustling Leaves of Paradise

In a hammock swaying, I take a nap,
A squirrel pops by, what a mishap!
He nibbles my snack, with eyes so wide,
I roll off giggling, what a wild ride!

The leaves above rustle with glee,
As bugs join in for a jamboree.
They cha-cha-cha, right on my nose,
Sneeze, oh dear! A shower of woes!

The sun peeks through, tickles my cheek,
And all around, the laughter peaks.
With every sigh, the world feels free,
Rustling leaves share their comedy spree.

In paradise where chuckles abound,
Every silly mishap is joyfully found.
With nature's rhythm, we dance and sway,
In this leafy laughter, we play all day.

Embrace of the Canopy

High up, the branches weave a plot,
As I swing down, oh what a shot!
A branch breaks free, it gives a crack,
I tumble down, but there's no lack!

Lizards mock me with their sly grin,
While vines above twist and spin.
I try to climb back to the heights,
Only to slip in nature's delights.

Here, the canopy holds its breath,
As I swing by, playing games of death.
Not really, just a flap and a spin,
In this green embrace, I always win.

Giggles swirl under the leafy dome,
In this canopy, I feel at home.
With every leap, new heights to find,
In the embrace of fun, I unwind.

The Shade of Solitude

In a hat that's too big, I sip lemonade,
A monkey steals snacks, I'm amazed and betrayed.
With leaves as my curtains, I sigh out a laugh,
Guess I've got a new friend, my snack-loving calf!

The breeze winks at me, it's trying to tease,
While birds in a chorus sing songs of lost keys.
I dance with a crab, it's all in good fun,
And maybe I'm done, or perhaps just begun.

The sun takes a break, the shadows stretch long,
While I contemplate life, like a lost little song.
With each passing hour, I tell jokes to the bugs,
They laugh at my puns, or just give me shrugs!

So here in my haven, I'll giggle and play,
With laughter my armor, and joy on display.
Who needs a grand throne when a leaf is just right?
In my sanctuary, I'm the queen of the night!

Tropical Reveries

Palm fronds a-swaying, I take off my shoes,
The sand tickles toes, oh, what lovely views!
A toucan appears with a fruit in its beak,
It drops it on me—oh, what a fine streak!

The waves play a tune, like a band made of cats,
Who knew they could strum with their furry little hats?
While dolphins do flips, with splashes and spins,
I'm laughing so hard, I forget where I've been.

A crab in a bow tie waltzes by, oh dear,
To a salsa tune, he brings the whole crew near.
With shells for maracas, they dance in a line,
A celebration of joy, everything's just fine!

As sun-kissed hours blend softly with light,
This paradise party could last through the night.
With laughter and music, my spirit takes flight,
In this tropical dream, everything's out of sight!

Plover's Flight Over Canopies

A plover flies high, with a hat made of clay,
I chuckle aloud at its stylish display.
With wings spread so wide, it zips like a dart,
Waving down below like a feathered sweetheart.

As shadows grow long, and the sky turns to gold,
I spot something swimming—could it be an old toad?
But it's just a flip-flop that's gone for a ride,
How's that for a tale of a footwear pride?

The breeze whispers secrets through branches above,
While crickets compose a sweet song filled with love.
I join in their chorus, all off-key and bold,
In this symphony sweet, I feel young and old.

So come join the fun under canopies wide,
With laughter like bubbles, let worries subside.
A dance in the shadows, a jig in the light,
A day full of mischief, and all things feel right!

Lush Embrace

In a tangle of vines, I find my new chair,
With leaves for a cushion, I sink without care.
A parrot recites my grocery list wrong,
It thinks we should party; it's right all along!

The sun giggles down while a lizard performs,
A stand-up routine that breaks all the norms.
With punchlines and puns, it captures the crowd,
Even clouds start to chuckle—are they too proud?

Seashells on the beach wear hats made of foam,
Telling tales of the sea when they're far from home.
With tides that tease gently, my worries drift out,
In this lush little world, there's no reason to pout.

So here's to the frolic, to sunshine and cheer,
In this overgrown jungle, let's dance without fear.
With laughter as currency, I'm rich more than gold,
In this vibrant embrace, we find joy uncontrolled!

The Sway of Solitude

In the shade, I take a seat,
Sipping drinks, a sweet retreat.
A seagull steals my sandwich snack,
I chase him off, but he won't pack!

Lizards strut, their tails on show,
Mocking me, just like a pro.
I laugh as they prance with grace,
While I'm stuck in this slow race.

Sunshine dances on the sand,
I drop my hat, not as I planned.
A crab scuttles with a grin,
Stealing my towel, oh what a win!

I wave to folks who wave back slow,
Is that a smile or just a glow?
Here in this quirky, sunny land,
Life's a joke and it's quite grand.

A Nest in Paradise

Up in the branches, birds all chirp,
Building nests, while I just burp.
They giggle at my beach ball flip,
I tumble down, it's quite the trip!

Squirrels stop and stare in shock,
As I attempt to take a walk.
My flip-flops squeak, they sound so loud,
Like a drum in my own little crowd.

A coconut drops, I duck and weave,
The little critters can't believe.
I throw a shell right back in fun,
But all it hits is my own sun!

With laughter echoing through the day,
I sip my mocktail, feel the sway.
In my silly, sunny place,
Life's a nest of joy and grace.

Cerulean Dreams and Sandy Footprints

The ocean waves, they wave hello,
I wave back, but off I go!
Stepping lightly on the shore,
A seagull swoops, then I hit the floor!

My footprints trail, a comical dance,
As jellyfish float, a weird romance.
I dodge a wave, miss by a strand,
Splash from a squawking, wet brown band.

Kites in the sky, like my dreams take flight,
I laugh at my hat taking off with fright.
It twirls and it swirls, like a wild kite,
All around me, what a sight!

Cerulean skies and sandy toes,
Each slip-and-slide a laughter grows.
In this paradise where moments gleam,
I drift through life, living my dream.

Warmth Wrapped in Green

Mangoes drop like bombs of fun,
I catch one too late, oh run!
Sticky fingers, what a treat,
I dance with joy, and dodge my feet!

A parrot thinks it can out-sing,
While locals laugh and join the fling.
I twist and shout, take a spin,
The palm fronds cheer, let the games begin!

Sunburnt cheeks and giggles bright,
I lose my shades, it's quite the sight.
In green embrace, I find my groove,
Feeling young, with every move.

This place is zany, full of cheer,
Old friends wave when they come near.
Wrapped in warmth, my heart's agleam,
Life's a play, a sunny dream.

www.ingramcontent.com/pod-product-compliance
Lightning Source LLC
Chambersburg PA
CBHW072123070526
44585CB00016B/1542